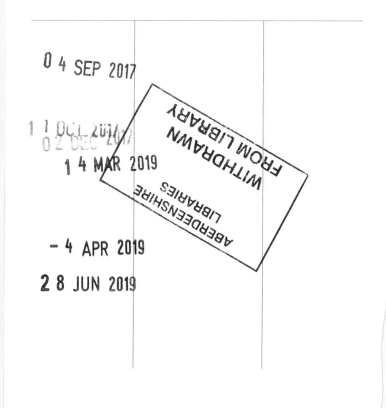

WHERE'S HORRID HENRY?

Francesca Simon

Orion
Children's Books

ORION CHILDREN'S BOOKS

First published in Great Britain in 2016
by Hodder and Stoughton
This paperback edition first published in Great Britain in 2017
by Hodder and Stoughton

1 3 5 7 9 10 8 6 4 2

A CIP catalogue record for this book
is available from the British Library.

ISBN 978 1 5101 0129 6

Printed and bound in China

The paper and board used in this book are from well-managed forests
and other responsible sources.

Orion Children's Books
An imprint of
Hachette Children's Group
Part of Hodder and Stoughton
Carmelite House
50 Victoria Embankment
London EC4Y 0DZ

An Hachette UK Company
www.hachette.co.uk
www.hachettechildrens.co.uk

www.horridhenry.co.uk

HEY PURPLE HAND GANG!

Are you ready to test your super spotting skills with my amazing search-and-find adventures? Be warned – some of them are really horrid!

Good luck!

Henry

What's lost?

Henry's fiendish friends and evil enemies have each lost one of their favourite possessions – they're listed throughout the book, see if you can spot them!

But wait, there's even more to look for! Can you spy Henry's awesome best presents ever?

Mega Whirl Goo Shooter

Super Soaker 2000

Whoopee Cushion

The Smellie Bellies' Greatest Hits CD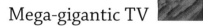

Mega-gigantic TV

Bugle Blast Boots

Dungeon Drink Kit

Roller Bowlers

How about Perfect Peter's stupid boring awful nappy baby wish list?

Colouring pencils

Books

Daffy and her Dancing Daisies Greatest Hits CD

Fluff Puff the Sheep

And keep your eyes peeled for fiendish fowl, Dolores the Chicken!

Don't forget ME, I'm hiding somewhere on every page!

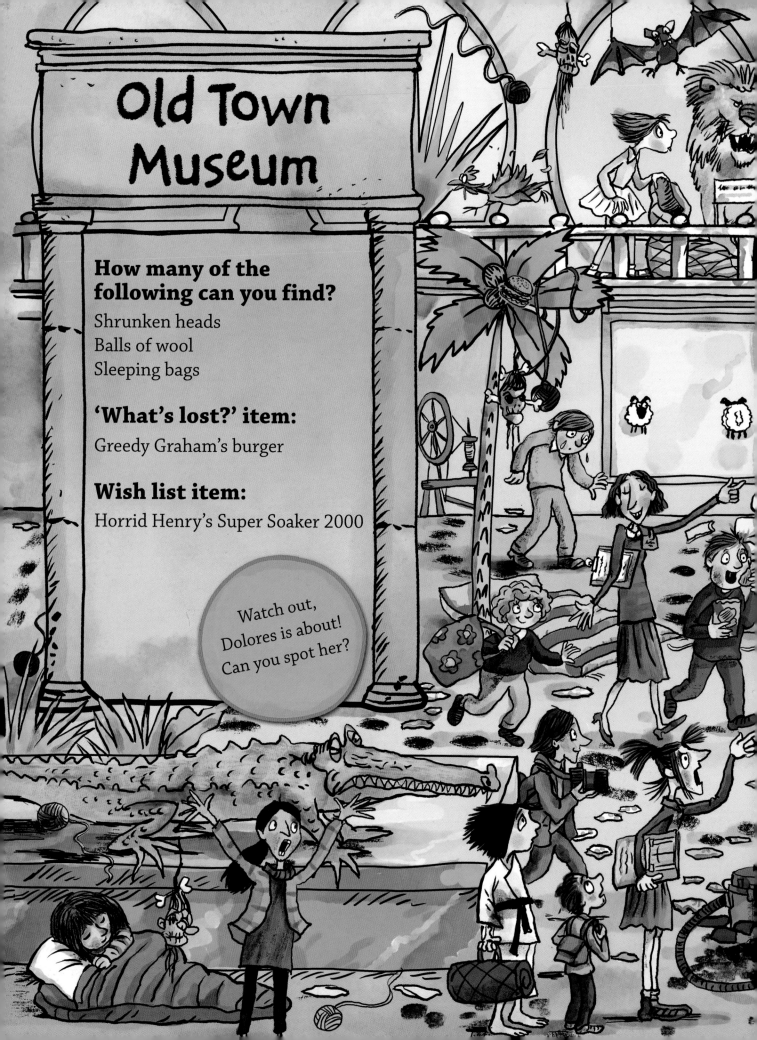

Christmas Chaos

How many of the following can you find?

Stockings
Christmas crackers
Scarves

'What's lost?' item:

Rude Ralph's Purple Hand Gang flag

Wish list item:

Horrid Henry's Roller
Bowlers

Hopefully Dad doesn't mistake Dolores the chicken for a turkey! Find her, quick!

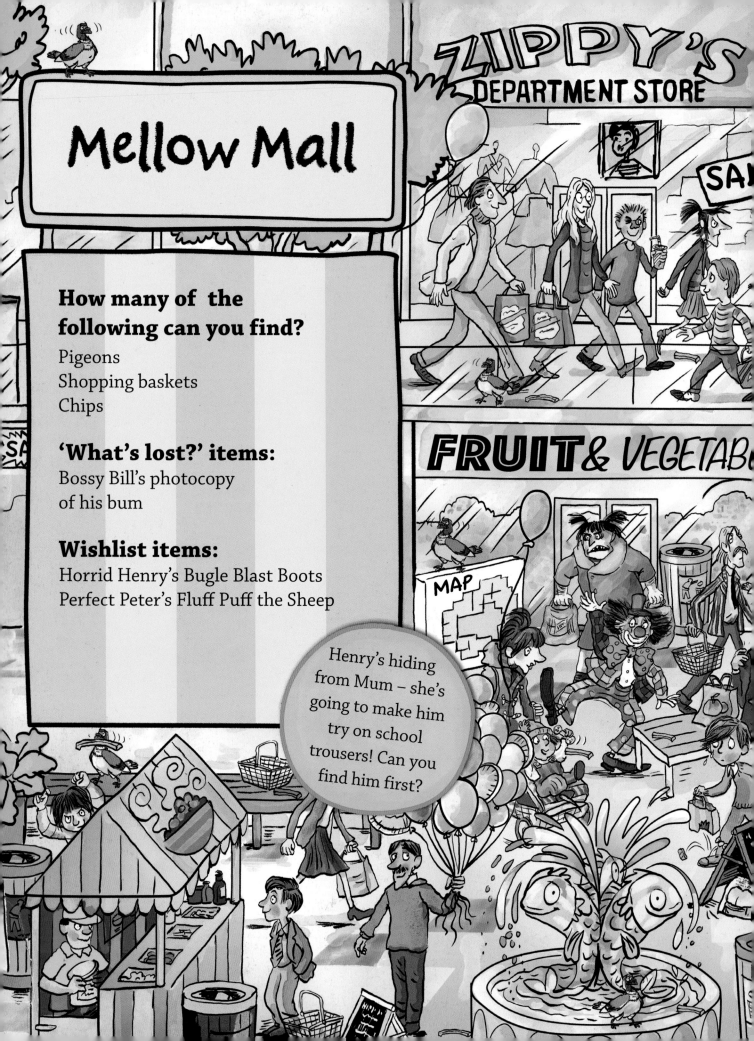

Mellow Mall

How many of the following can you find?
Pigeons
Shopping baskets
Chips

'What's lost?' items:
Bossy Bill's photocopy of his bum

Wishlist items:
Horrid Henry's Bugle Blast Boots
Perfect Peter's Fluff Puff the Sheep

Henry's hiding from Mum – she's going to make him try on school trousers! Can you find him first?

ZIPPY'S DEPARTMENT STORE

SA

FRUIT & VEGETAB

MAP

School Sports Day

How many of the following can you find?

Eggs and spoons
Flags
Medals

'What's lost?' item:

Horrid Henry's teddy, Mr Kill

Wishlist item:

Perfect Peter's pile of boring school books

Dolores the chicken loves an egg and spoon race. Find her before she steals all of the eggs!

Camp Cramp

How many of the following can you find?
Toilet rolls
Bugs
Sausages

'What's lost?' item:
Singing Soraya's microphone

Wishlist item:
Horrid Henry's *Smellie Bellies' Greatest Hits* CD

Quick, hide! Henry's spotted Miss Battle-Axe by the loos – can you find his sneaky spying spot?

Horrid Henry's Haunted House

How many of the following can you find?
Spiders
Skulls
Bats

'What's lost?' item:
Perfect Peter's handkerchief

Wishlist item:
Horrid Henry's Dungeon
Drink Kit

Zombies, ghosts,
Moody Margaret –
aargh, the terror!
Plus, fiendish fowl
Dolores is still on the
loose, beware!

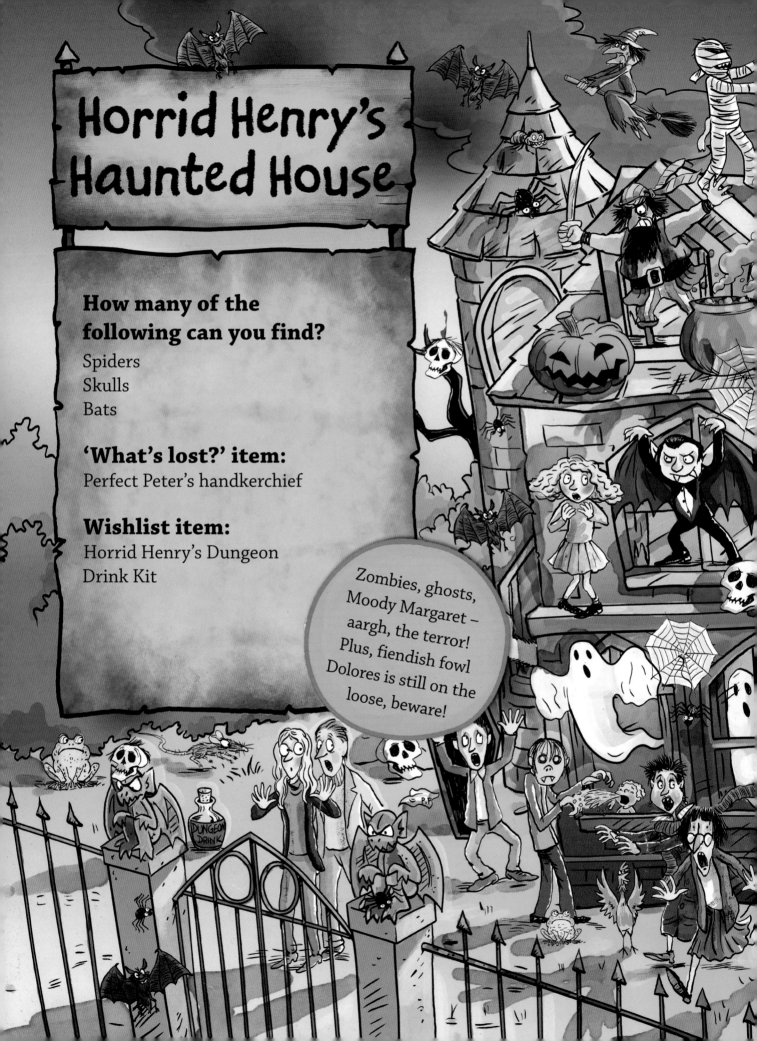

Answers

Here's Horrid Henry!

There are:
11 presents, 7 slices of cake, 11 balloons, 4 jellies

Miss Battle-Axe's whistle is on the floor next to Greedy Graham

Henry's whoopee cushion is on the sofa

Here's Horrid Henry!

There are:
10 raffle tickets, 5 bags of crisps, 3 lunchboxes

Moody Margaret's trumpet is on top of the bunting

Henry's mega-gigantic TV is under the cake stall

There are:
10 shrunken heads, 11 balls of wool, 9 sleeping bags

Greedy Graham's burger is in the palm tree

Henry's Super-Soaker is under the rocking chair

There are:
7 stockings, 10 Christmas crackers, 4 scarves

Rude Ralph's Purple Hand Gang flag is on the Christmas tree

Henry's Roller Bowlers are next to Moody Margaret

There are:
10 buckets, 12 shells,
9 crabs, 9 ice creams

Aerobic Al's trainers are near Lazy Linda

Perfect Peter's colouring pencils are under Granny's foot

Here's Horrid Henry!

Sandy Bottom Beach

How many of the following can you find?
Buckets
Shells
Crabs
Ice creams

'What's lost?' item:
Aerobic Al's trainers

Wishlist item:
Perfect Peter's colouring pencils

Blecccch, Henry hates the beach. Luckily he's found the perfect spot to spend the day …

Here's Horrid Henry!

Scruff's Pet Show

SCRUFF'S PET SHOW

How many of the following can you find?
Rosettes
Bones
Leads

'What's lost?' item:
Perfect Peter's cello

Wishlist items:
Perfect Peter's *Daffy and her Dancing Daisies Greatest Hits* CD
Horrid Henry's Mega Whirl Goo Shooter

With so many animals running wild, keeping an eye out for deadly Dolores is going to be tricky …

There are: 6 rosettes, 12 bones, 5 leads

Perfect Peter's cello is on top of the red tunnel

Perfect Peter's *Daffy and her Dancing Daisies Greatest Hits* CD is next to Dolores the chicken

Henry's Mega Whirl Goo Shooter is under the 'Scruff's Pet Show' banner

Here's
Horrid Henry!

Mellow Mall

How many of the following can you find?
Pigeons
Shopping baskets
Chips

'What's lost?' items:
Bossy Bill's photocopy of his bum

Wishlist items:
Horrid Henry's Bugle Blast Boots
Perfect Peter's Fluff Puff the Sheep

Henry's hiding from Mum – she's going to make him try on school trousers! Can you find him first?

There are:
11 pigeons, 8 shopping baskets, 15 chips

Bossy Bill's photocopy of his bum is under the sandwich board

Henry's Bugle Blast Boots are beside the food tent

Perfect Peter's Fluff Puff the Sheep is outside the shoe shop

Here's
Horrid Henry!

There are: 6 eggs and spoons, 11 flags, 5 medals

Henry's teddy, Mr Kill, is next to the red flag at the top of the racetrack

Perfect Peter's pile of school books is next to Greedy Graham

School Sports Day

How many of the following can you find?
Egg and spoons
Flags
Medals

'What's lost?' item:
Horrid Henry's teddy
Mr Kill

Wishlist item:
Perfect Peter's pile of boring school books

Dolores the chicken loves an egg and spoon race. Find her before she steals all of the eggs!

Here's Horrid Henry!

Camp Cramp

How many of the following can you find?
Toilet rolls
Bugs
Sausages

'What's lost?' item:
Singing Soraya's microphone

Wishlist item:
Horrid Henry's *Smellie Bellies' Greatest Hits* CD

Quick, hide! Henry's spotted Miss Battle-Axe by the loos – can you find his sneaky spying spot?

There are:
10 toilet rolls, 10 bugs, 10 sausages

Singing Soraya's microphone is in Jolly Josh's tent

Henry's *Smellie Bellie's Greatest Hits* CD is in the back window of the car

Horrid Henry's Haunted House

How many of the following can you find?
Spiders
Skulls
Bats

'What's lost?' item:
Perfect Peter's hankerchief

Wishlist item:
Horrid Henry's Dungeon Drink

Zombies, ghosts, Moody Margaret – aargh, the terror! Plus, fiendish fowl Dolores is still on the loose, beware!

There are:
15 spiders, 8 skulls, 9 bats

Perfect Peter's handkerchief is behind Dad

Henry's Dungeon Drink Kit is next to Mum

Here's Horrid Henry!